PRAY STRENGTHEN

MARRIAGES AND FAMILIES

Apostle Stephen A. Garner

Rivers Publishing Company
Stephen A. Garner Ministries
P.O. Box 1545, Bolingbrook, IL 60440
E-mail: sagarnerministries@gmail.com
www.sagministries.com

Printed in the United States of America

TABLE OF CONTENTS

INTRODUCTION

One of the greatest duties the believer in Christ has is to speak what we believe. God's Word is the only source for accurate belief systems for the believer. The apostle Paul in the referenced verse is challenging the Corinthian believers to practice speaking what God's Word says. I have found this to be a very valuable discipline in my personal life. The Lord declares in John 6 that the words He speaks are spirit and life.

This booklet is loaded with spirit-inspired prayers that will certainly ignite a passion in you to make prayers, decrees, declarations and proclamations for your marriage and family. Utilize them as often as needed or until desired results manifest. I come into agreement with you now for marital breakthrough and family success.

2 Corinthians 4:13 KJV
We having the same spirit of faith, according as it is written, I believed, and therefore have I spoken; we also believe, and therefore speak;

2 Corinthians 4:13 Message
We're not keeping this quiet, not on your life. Just like the psalmist who wrote, "I believed it, so I said it," we say what we believe.

2 Corinthians 4:13 Complete Jewish Bible
The *Tanakh* says, **"I trusted, therefore I spoke."** Since we have that same Spirit who enables us to trust, we also trust and therefore speak;

PRAYERS FOR BINDING AND LOOSING MARRIAGES

Matthew 16:19 (KJV)
And I will give unto thee the keys of the kingdom of heaven: and whatsoever thou shalt **bind on earth** shall be **bound in heaven**: and whatsoever thou shalt **loose on earth** shall be **loosed in heaven.**

Matthew 18:18 (KJV)
Verily I say unto you, Whatsoever ye shall **bind on earth** shall be **bound in heaven**: and whatsoever ye shall **loose on earth** shall be **loosed in heaven**.

Bind (G1210 deō) to bind, fasten with chains, to throw into chains, to bind, put under obligation, of the law, duty etc; to forbid, prohibit, declare to be illicit.

Loose (G3089 lyō) to loose any person (or thing) tied or fastened, to loose one bound, i.e. to unbind, release from bonds, set free, to loosen, undo, dissolve, anything bound, tied, or compacted together, to do away with, to deprive of authority, whether by precept or act

1)   I loose my marriage from every satanic vice and strategy to abort our destiny together in Jesus Name.

2)   I bind all demons of anger rooted in immaturity and arrested development in Jesus Name.

3)   I loose peace and prosperity over my marriage.

4) I bind all demons of pride and contention.

5) I bind all arguing, quarreling and strife in Jesus Name.

6) I loose godly wisdom upon my marriage and I decree wisdom is destroying every beast assigned against my marriage.

7) I bind all spirits of un-forgiveness and torment against my marriage.

8) I loose sanctification and holiness over my marriage.

9) I bind all demons assigned to release financial hardship and economic failure in my marriage.

10) I loose godly wisdom for financial savvy and maturity in my marriage.

11) I bind all assignments of covenant breaking spirits of divorce, separation and marital destruction in Jesus Name.

12) I loose patience and grace to suffer long in my marriage in Jesus Name.

13) I loose divine insight for an acceptable future concerning my marriage in Jesus Name.

14) I bind all self-righteousness and egotism that would seek to work through me and undermine God's plan for my marriage.

15) I bind all deception and demonic illusions assigned against my marriage. I decree obstructions from both the visible and invisible realms are neutralized by the blood of Jesus.

16) I bind every force of darkness present to mar our vision concerning the handiwork of God in our marriage.

17) I loose grace in my marriage to operate with greater yielding and merging to God and to one another in Jesus Name.

18) I bind all fatigue, insensitivity, laziness and carnality assigned against my marriage in Jesus Name.

19) I loose my marriage from any forms of idolatry in Jesus Name.

20) I loose divine order and clarity concerning roles and responsibilities.

21) I bind all demonic communication through grievous words and demon-inspired dialog, which stirs anger.

22) I loose purpose and passion into my marriage for breakthrough and excellence.

23) I bind all demons that would drive wedges into my marriage.

24) I bind all demons that would seek to control my marriage through manipulation and confusion.

25) I loose righteousness over our minds. Lord I grant you access to govern our thoughts by righteousness in Jesus Name.

26) I loose humility to stay the course and remain engaged with my spouse regardless of how I feel.

27) I loose generational blessings over my marriage. I decree these blessings flow into future generations. My grand and great grand and great great grandchildren are set up for success because of the foundation of my marriage in Jesus Name.

28) I bind every satanic strategy activated to wreak havoc in my marriage through employment problems and infirmity in Jesus Name.

29) I bind all attacks of darkness against my children desiring to strain my marriage in Jesus Name.

30) I bind all spirits of familiarity with my spouse seeking to overthrow my marriage.

31) I decree I dwell with my spouse according to knowledge and I loose our inheritances of grace for life in Jesus Name.

PROCLAMATIONS FOR OUR FAMILY

Proclamation: an official statement or announcement made by a person of power or by a government.

Ezra 8:21 (KJV)
Then **I proclaimed (Ezra)** a fast there, at the river of Ahava, that we might afflict ourselves before our God, to seek of him a right way for us, and for our little ones, and for all our substance.

Revelation 5:2 (KJV)
And I saw a **strong angel proclaiming** with a loud voice, Who is worthy to open the book, and to loose the seals thereof?

1) I proclaim fruitfulness over my FAMILY in every assignment and mandate ordained for us by God. I renounce every destructive plan of Satan and proclaim restoration to fruitfulness in Jesus Name.

2) I proclaim breakthrough in my FAMILY. I decree we overcome every obstacle and obstruction to our success. I decree we advance and the Breaker goes before us in Jesus Name.

3) I proclaim divine health and healing over my FAMILY. I decree every sickness and disease known to man shall not live in the bodies of the members of my household in Jesus Name.

4) I renounce all destructive assignments established in

my bloodline and FAMILY. I decree through the shed blood of Jesus every assignment of damnation, ruin and failure breaks off our lives in Jesus Name.

5) I proclaim social advances over my FAMILY and household. I decree success in relationships, education, employment, entrepreneurship and destiny exploits in Jesus Name.

6) I proclaim grace to overcome and subdue every barrier to progress. All strategies, plots, traps, plans and subtleties of Satan are rooted out. Grace increases in my household and FAMILY in Jesus Name.

7) I proclaim restoration over my FAMILY from all setbacks, failures, breakdowns, meltdowns, mishaps, misuse and mediocrity assigned against us in Jesus Name.

8) I proclaim increased financial capacity and freedom over my FAMILY. I decree my FAMILY is loosed from all assignments of lack, insufficiency, poverty, scarcity, leanness, debt and assignments to make us destitute. I decree that we are liberal in giving and the spirit of generosity rest upon us in the Name of Jesus.

9) I proclaim godly living and longevity over every member of my FAMILY. I rebuke all assignments of violence, accidents, premature death and wickedness. I decree my FAMILY prevails and thrives in righteousness.

10) I proclaim generational blessings over my FAMILY. Every work of curses and generational wickedness is subdued and overturned in Jesus Name.

11) I proclaim open heavens and access to the good

treasures of heaven. I decree they are flowing in and through my FAMILY in Jesus Name.

12) I proclaim the blessing of Naphtali over my FAMILY. I decree we are full of the blessing and satisfied with favor.

13) I proclaim the blessing of Joseph over my FAMILY. I decree we are planted by the water and refreshing is upon us, our vines shoot over walls and the dew of heaven is on my household to prosper us in Jesus Name.

14) I proclaim the power of God over my FAMILY. I decree my FAMILY is growing in the authority and ability of God.

15) I proclaim the glory and the weighty presence of God is increasing mightily in my domain and upon all who are joined to my loins for generations to come in Jesus Name.

16) I proclaim new levels of honor for God, Christ and His Church arising in the heart of every member of my FAMILY. I decree elevated levels of respect for the house of God increasing in us daily.

17) I proclaim largeness of heart is manifesting in my FAMILY. Our capacity to receive, dispense and be creative is expanding in Jesus Name.

18) I proclaim elevated levels of extreme obedience upon my FAMILY. I decree every dark strategy against us is broken in Jesus Name.

19) I proclaim consistency and faithfulness abounds in every member of my FAMILY and household towards

Christ and His Kingdom.

20) I proclaim divine wisdom and understanding upon my FAMILY. I decree godly wisdom is operating in every aspect of our lives in Jesus Name.

21) I proclaim increase in kindness and mercy upon my FAMILY in Jesus Name.

22) I proclaim an increase of sensitivity for the needs of one another in my FAMILY.

23) I declare my FAMILY is gaining momentum in overcoming setbacks and obstacles in Jesus Name.

24) My FAMILY thrives in loving and serving one another in Jesus Name.

25) I proclaim deliverance from every anti-prosperity pit where my FAMILY has been ensnared in Jesus Name.

26) I decree my FAMILY is liberated from all territorial influences connected to anti-family strongholds in Jesus Name.

27) I claim diplomatic immunity over my FAMILY as heirs of Gods Kingdom from all demonic plots, demonic influences and humanistic wisdom.

28) All strategies of demons seeking to ruin my FAMILY legacy due to vile practices and activity forbidden in God's Word is rooted out in Jesus Name.

29) I proclaim the redemptive power of the blood of Jesus over every member of my FAMILY in Jesus Name. I decree through the blood of Jesus, all demonic recruitments are defeated in Jesus Name.

30) I proclaim healthy practices; appetites and desires abound among the members of my FAMILY in Jesus Name.

PRAYERS FOR RENOUNCING POVERTY

Poverty: the state or condition of having little or no money, goods, or means of support; condition of being poor; deficiency of necessary or desirable ingredients, qualities, etc; scantiness, insufficiency

Proverbs 10:15 (KJV)
The rich man's wealth is his strong city: the destruction of the poor is their **poverty.**

1) I renounce every strategy of the enemy connected to financial ignorance and anti-covenant demons that seek to make poverty and leanness thrive against my purpose in life.

2) I renounce every enemy of increase and advancement in Jesus Name.

3) I loose myself from all ignorance and knowledge blocking strongholds concerning financial prosperity.

4) I renounce every mentality and mindset established in my family line that causes financial increase and breakthrough to remain at bay.

5) I renounce all fear connected to success and growth concerning natural and spiritual things.

6) I renounce every sanction and restraint spoken over my life that would seek to contain me through poor stewardship and financial instability in Jesus Name.

7) I break covenant with any and all verbal agreements designed to fortify poverty in my life in the Name of Jesus.

8) I come out of agreement with every work of destruction, despair, hopelessness and ruin linked to poverty. I sever the connections and proclaim freedom over my life.

9) I renounce allegiance to every taskmaster I've covenanted with and I loose increase over my life.

10) Lord break the brass heavens above me and the iron earth beneath.

11) I renounce every spend thrift spirit that seeks to hold me captive through lack of financial discipline in Jesus name.

12) I renounce every spirit of fear that rises when economic challenges manifest through systems and governments because of greed on their part. I decree You alone are my source.

13) Lord forgive me for any and all negligence concerning the seeds You put in my hands. I repent today for any and all misuse of money in Jesus Name.

14) Lord I ask You, for healing in my soul, from any and all roots of poverty. I decree You have redeemed me from the curse of poverty and lack.

15) I renounce all greed, covetousness and lust for things associated to poverty, lack and neediness assigned against me.

16) I renounce all pride that won't allow me to ask for help

and resources due to lack.

17) I break allegiance with all false humility rooted in poverty.

18) I renounce every vow and pledge to poverty rooted in religion and error.

19) I renounce the seed waster, fruit eater and increase destroyer assigned against my prosperity in the Name of Jesus.

20) I renounce every power of poverty that seeks to keep the windows of heaven closed over my life.

21) I close every door, every gate, every opening and access point to the spirit of poverty and lack against my life.

22) I break the operating capacity of poverty assigned against my life and I renounce every support system at work in my mind in the Name of Jesus! I decree I'm made for increase!

23) Lord, as I practice tithing, giving offerings, alms, first fruits and sacrificial giving, I ask you to judge and render ineffective every function of poverty assigned to shut me out of increase and abundance in the Name of Jesus!

24) I renounce all insufficiency, lack, infirmity, drought and famine against your mandate for me to prosper in life.

25) Lord, forgive me for every time I've closed my eyes and ears toward the needy. I repent for any refusal to help those whom I possessed the power to do good to

in Jesus Name.

26) I renounce all lies, false teachings and anti-prosperity spirits seeking to make my life void of your plans to prosper me.

27) I proclaim wisdom, favor and insight to move in multiple streams of income in Jesus Name.

28) I renounce all strongholds of poverty designed to rob me of dreams, strategies and insight into realms of expansion and increase.

29) I proclaim access to covenant wealth as a son/daughter of Abraham in Jesus Name.

PRAYERS FOR MARITAL VICTORY

Victory: success or triumph over an enemy in battle or war, an engagement ending in such triumph, the ultimate and decisive superiority in any battle or contest; a success or superior position achieved against any opponent, opposition or difficulty.

1 Corinthians 15:57 (KJV)
But thanks be to God, which giveth us the **VICTORY** through our Lord Jesus Christ.

1 Corinthians 15:57 (AMP)
But thanks be to God, Who gives us the **VICTORY** making us conquerors through our Lord Jesus Christ.

1) I pronounce the blessing of unity and oneness upon my marriage.

2) I declare respect for my spouse and godly reverence is thriving in my marriage.

3) I speak fruitfulness and success over my marriage. Every plan of flawed productivity is destroyed in the Name of Jesus.

4) I decree favor and abundance of love, accurate communication and harmony flows freely in my marriage in Jesus Name.

5) I release elevated levels of submission over my life to

serve and honor my spouse.

6) I break all demonic-inspired programs against my marriage and root out all strategies of failure.

7) I decree God's banner over my marriage is love.

8) I proclaim peace and freedom from all quarreling, arguing and marital sabotage in Jesus Name.

9) I forbid any and all negative effects from past relationships, hurts, wounds and traumatic experiences to access to my marital life today.

10) All demonic networks of lust, perversion and adultery are displaced and rendered inoperative against my marriage.

11) All spirits of seduction and illegal conversations are aborted through the blood of Jesus.

12) I pronounce success, longevity and divine health upon my marriage in Jesus Name.

13) All negative outside interference from in-laws, co-workers, friends and the saints is cut-off.

14) I pronounce honor over my marriage and all root system of dishonor are removed by the power of God.

15) I command every stone of reproach to be rolled away from grave openings where my marriage has been buried by false burdens, deceit and confusion. I decree my marriage rises from every grave, pit and tomb in Jesus Name.

16) All cords of hurt, disappointments and setbacks

connecting my marriage to defeat are severed and cast away in Jesus Name.

17) My marriage shall not be a statistic of failure, but one of success, righteousness, accuracy and legacy in Jesus Name.

18) Stability and soundness flows in my marriage and all streams of dysfunction are under intense drought in Jesus Name.

19) Every tactic of satan to drive me to minimize or devalue my spouse is subdued in the Name of Jesus.

20) I decree every demonic assignment of sickness and genetic disorders connected to infirmity is defeated. Health and longevity is the portion of my marriage.

21) All invisible barriers positioned against the progress of my marriage are broken in the Name of Jesus.

22) Every undermining strategy against my marriage through stress, anger and discontentedness are neutralized by the blood of Jesus.

23) I decree honor for the vows I made towards my spouse in Jesus Name.

24) I decree my marriage thrives because we honor our covenant with God and our covenant with each other.

25) I speak the goodness of God upon my marriage and all demonic agencies of sorrow and hardship flee from us in Jesus Name.

26) I speak new levels of victory in unity and agreement over my spouse and me in Jesus Name.

27) Husbands Only - I receive grace and wisdom to minister to the needs of my wife in the areas of affection, conversation, transparency, financial security and family commitment in the Name of Jesus.

28) Wives Only – I receive grace and wisdom to minister to the needs of my husband in the areas of sex, friendship, affirmation, honor and respect in the Name of Jesus.

29) Husbands Only – I decree grace is upon me to love my wife, embrace her input, cherish her, make decisions for the well-being of my marriage and initiate actions that will cause my marriage to excel in Jesus Name.

30) Wives Only – I decree grace is upon me to be a wise helper for my husband. I receive grace to submit and comply with his mission. I will uphold him, honor him and pray for him in Jesus Name.

PRAYERS FOR MARITAL ALIGNMENT IN CHRIST

Alignment: the proper adjustment of the components of an electronic circuit, machine, etc., for coordinated functioning; state of agreement or cooperation among persons, groups, nations, etc., with a common cause or viewpoint.

Christ is our Chief Corner Stone and Head of His people. Alignment with Him is vital to fulfilling any assignment ordained by Him. Marriage is ordained of God. If we are to function in a healthy context, with our spouses we must stay aligned, with the One who has power to sustain us. May your marriage and family life be engulfed with new inspiration as you discover the benefits of being IN CHRIST.

Romans 8:1 (KJV)
There is therefore now no condemnation to them which are IN CHRIST JESUS, who walk not after the flesh, but after the Spirit.

1)   I speak alignment with Christ over my marriage today. I decree no guilt, shame or condemnation shall cast any shadows over my marriage because I am in Christ. My walk is after the Spirit and not after the flesh.

Romans 8:2 (KJV)
For the law of the Spirit of life IN CHRIST JESUS hath made me free from the law of sin and death.

2)   I decree freedom from sin and all its damnable affects over my marriage. For the law of the Spirit of life in Christ hath liberated my marriage from the law of sin

and death in Jesus Name.

Romans 8:38-39 (KJV)
For I am persuaded, that neither death, nor life, nor angels, nor principalities, nor powers, nor things present, nor things to come, 39 Nor height, nor depth, nor any other creature, shall be able to separate us from the love of God, which is IN CHRIST JESUS our Lord.

3)   I proclaim steadfastness in the love of God, which is in Christ Jesus over my marriage. I declare we are empowered to stand in our covenant together, free from any separation anxieties and fears. Nothing shall separate us from you Lord.

Romans 12:5 (KJV)
So we, being many, are one body IN CHRIST, and every one members one of another.

4)   I confess new levels of connectivity and oneness in my marriage because we are aligned with Christ.

1 Corinthians 1:30 (KJV)
But of him are ye IN CHRIST JESUS, who of God is made unto us wisdom, and righteousness, and sanctification, and redemption:

5)   I proclaim elevated levels of sanctification are upon my marriage. I decree my marriage is set apart and full of glory because we are in Christ.

1 Corinthians 4:10 (KJV)
We are fools for Christ's sake, but ye are wise IN CHRIST; we are weak, but ye are strong; ye are honourable, but we are despised.

6) I confess godly wisdom over my marriage. I decree we are strong and honorable to one another because we are in Christ.

1 Corinthians 15:22 (KJV)
For as in Adam all die, even so IN CHRIST shall all be made alive.

7) I declare the power of Christ the Anointed One over my marriage. I fall out of agreement with the lineage of Adam rooted in death and separation. I decree my marriage is alive in Christ.

2 Corinthians 2:14 (KJV)
Now thanks be unto God, which always causeth us to triumph IN CHRIST, and maketh manifest the savour of his knowledge by us in every place.

8) God I give thanks unto You, for You cause my marriage triumph in Christ and the fragrance of Your presence is manifesting through my marriage in Jesus Name.

2 Corinthians 2:17 (KJV)
For we are not as many, which corrupt the word of God: but as of sincerity, but as of God, in the sight of God speak we IN CHRIST.

9) I renounce all powers of corruption that would seek to minimize my marital mandate in Christ. I speak sincerity in handling the Word of God over my spouse and me.

2 Corinthians 3:14 (KJV)
But their minds were blinded: for until this day remaineth the same veil untaken away in the reading of the Old Testament; which veil is done away IN CHRIST.

10) Today every barrier, obstruction, hindrance and veil in my mind against the Word, concerning my marriage is divinely displaced, for in Christ the hindrances are taken away. I receive your Word with clarity and purpose for my marriage in Jesus Name.

2 Corinthians 5:17 (KJV)
Therefore if any man be IN CHRIST, he is a new creature: old things are passed away; behold, all things are become new.

11) I decree my marriage is in Christ and all things have become new. Yesterday's failures and its frustrations have passed away and all things in our covenant are new in Jesus Name!

2 Corinthians 11:3 (KJV)
But I fear, lest by any means, as the serpent beguiled Eve through his subtilty, so your minds should be corrupted from the simplicity that is IN CHRIST.

12) Lord, empower me and my spouse, to never stray from the principles of your Word and its simplicity; which is in Christ.

Ephesians 2:6 (KJV)
And hath raised us up together, and made us sit together in heavenly places IN CHRIST JESUS:

13) I decree every cord and connection to carnal mindsets is broken off my marriage. I decree we rise to our heavenly position in Christ.

Ephesians 2:10 (KJV)
For we are his workmanship, created IN CHRIST JESUS unto good works, which God hath before ordained that we should walk in them.

14) I declare my marriage is the workmanship of Christ. I proclaim ingenuity, innovation and creativity in my marriage. I decree we walk in ordained places because of Christ.

Ephesians 2:13 (KJV)
But now IN CHRIST JESUS ye, who sometimes were far off are made nigh by the blood of Christ.

15) I decree that through the blood of Christ the drawing power of God rest upon my marriage. Lord draw us into new experiences and encounters of loving You and one another in Jesus Name.

PRAYERS FOR OUR CHILDREN

Our children are the links to our future. Through them our values, morals and lifestyles will continue impacting generations, even those yet to be born. God is concerned about the generations and holds our sons and daughters in high regards. With so much being at stake as it relates to our sons and daughters, we need to pray for them without ceasing. May immeasurable fervor, clarity and accuracy be released through your prayers on behalf of your children.

1) Lord, You declared though the wicked join forces they shall not go unpunished, but the seed of the righteous shall be delivered. I claim deliverance for my seed in Jesus Name. –Proverbs 11:21

2) I decree your angels encamp around my children and angelic activity increases on their behalf. -Psalm 34:7

3) Every plot to cause their demise is overthrown and every crafty device programmed against their safety is rendered ineffective in the Name of Jesus. – Job 5:12

4) I proclaim divine protection over my children and decree they dwell under the shadow of the Almighty. – Psalm 91:1

5) I decree that You are a wall around my seed and fire in their midst in Jesus Name. –Zechariah 2:5

6) Lord I ask you to strive with those who strive with my children and fight against those that fight against them. You are my children's shield and buckler. – Psalm 35:1

7) Father thank You for accurate people in the lives of my children. Every wolf in sheep clothing is driven from their presence.

8) I renounce every strategy of Satan against my seed designed to forge ungodly soul ties in Jesus Name.

9) I decree my seed possess wisdom to make calculated decisions regarding their friends in Jesus Name.

10) I bind demons of Delilah assigned against my son and demons of Casanova assigned against my daughter in Jesus Name.

11) I decree all advocates of evil and wickedness assigned against my children are neutralized and impotent in their assignment against my seed in Jesus Name.

12) I decree the God-ordained relationship for my children will not be aborted, but come into full fruition.

13) Father, release elevated desire in my seed to serve and follow after you.

14) I proclaim passionate pursuit for Christ manifesting in the life of my children.

15) I decree the gift of divine hunger operating in my seed for God and His Word in Jesus Name.

16) I decree my children are awakened to the realities of Christ and the convicting power of Your love and presence is overwhelming them in Jesus Name.

17) I speak open heavens and open vision over my seed. I decree that through them the Kingdom of God shall be extended.

18) Father, cause Your ways to be known to my children and cause Your Name to be manifest against every enemy assigned against their walk with You.

19) I declare academic excellence over my children. Every negative word spoken against them to hinder their academic exploits falls to the ground in Jesus Name.

20) I decree that my children increase in learning and in knowledge.

21) Every obstruction to my children's academic accomplishments is overcome in the Name of Jesus.

22) I declare my sons and daughters have a love and zeal for knowledge. I decree they excel and rise to greater degrees of education in Jesus Name.

23) I decree my seed acquires the proper skill sets to advance in technology, math and science.

24) I claim scholarships, grants, merit money and hidden funds for my children's education is manifesting now in Jesus Name.

25) I pray for the proper teachers, coaches, counselors and professionals to come into my children's life in Jesus Name.

26) Father I ask You to fortify my seed in their identity in Jesus Name.

27) I rebuke all assignment of perversion, gender confusion and identity distorting demons in Jesus Name.

28) I take authority over demons positioned against my seed to rob them of their sexual innocence and purity. All molesters, pedophiles, sexually depraved, lustful people and demons are bound in Jesus Name.

29) Every systemic release of sexual uncleanness is rooted out of my child presence in Jesus Name.

30) Lord You have declared that You're able to keep that which I commit unto You. I commit my children unto You in Jesus Name.

31) Father, establish Your covenant of healing in the life of my seed.

32) I claim healing from every generational work of infirmity in my bloodline. I decree infirmity will not traffic into the life of my seed.

33) I rebuke all genetic disorders and assignments to ruin the health of my children in the Name of Jesus.

34) I declare divine health over my seed. Lord arise in their midst with healing in Your wings.

35) Lord, You have blessed the bread and water of my seed and taken sickness from their midst in Jesus Name.

36) I renounce every work of infirmity assigned against my seed. I claim healing from any and all disorders in Jesus Name.

37) I decree the rebuke of the Lord over my seeds' cardiovascular system, nervous system, skeletal system, digestive system, endocrine system, respiratory system and muscular system in the Name of Jesus.

38) I decree all demonic diagnosis over my seeds health is cancelled and disannulled in Jesus Name.

39) I decree my children prosper and are in health as their souls are prospering in Jesus Name.

More Great Resources from
Stephen A. Garner Ministries

Books

- Apostolic Pioneering
- Benefits of Praying in Tongues
- Exposing the Spirit of Anger
- Fundamentals of Deliverance 101, Revised & Expanded
- Ministering Spirits: "Engaging the Angelic Realm"
- Pray Without Ceasing, Special Edition
- Restoring Prophetic Watchmen
- Deliver Us From Evil
- Essentials of the Prophetic, Revised & Expanded
- The Kingdom of God: A Believer's Guide to Kingdom Living
- Kingdom Prayer
- Prayers, Decrees and Confessions for Wisdom
- Prayers, Decrees and Confessions for Favour & Grace
- Prayers, Decrees and Confessions for Prosperity
- Prayers, Decrees and Confessions for Increase
- Prayers, Decrees and Confessions for Righteousness, Revised & Expanded
- Prayers, Decrees and Confessions for Goodness
- Prayers, Decrees and Confessions for Power

CD's

- Prayers For The Nations
- Prayers Against Python & Witchcraft
- Prayers Of Healing & Restoration
- Prayers of Renunciation and Deliverance
- Thy Kingdom Come
- The Glory
- Latter Rain
- Overcoming Spirits of Terrorism
- Songs of Intercession
- The Spirit of the Breaker
- The Fear of the Lord

CONTACT INFORMATION
STEPHEN A. GARNER MINISTRIES
P.O. BOX 1545, BOLINGBROOK, IL 60440
EMAIL: SAGARNERMINISTRIES@GMAIL.COM
WWW.SAGMINISTRIES.COM

89603654R00020

Made in the USA
Lexington, KY
31 May 2018